What's inside?

This book tells you lots of exciting things about your body. Inside your body, you have soft parts and hard parts that all do special jobs. They work together to help you to speak and move, eat and drink, play and sleep!

 4 My body

 6 Bones

 **8** Run and jump

 10 Inside my body

 12 Playing in the park

 14 My face

 16 See and hear

 18 Touch and feel

 20 Taste and smell

 22 Keeping well

 24 Fun at the beach

 26 Story

 31 Puzzles

 32 Index

My body

Your body is amazing! It's made up of lots of different parts, inside a stretchy covering of skin. Girls and boys look different from each other but their bodies work in the same ways. Can you name the main parts of your body?

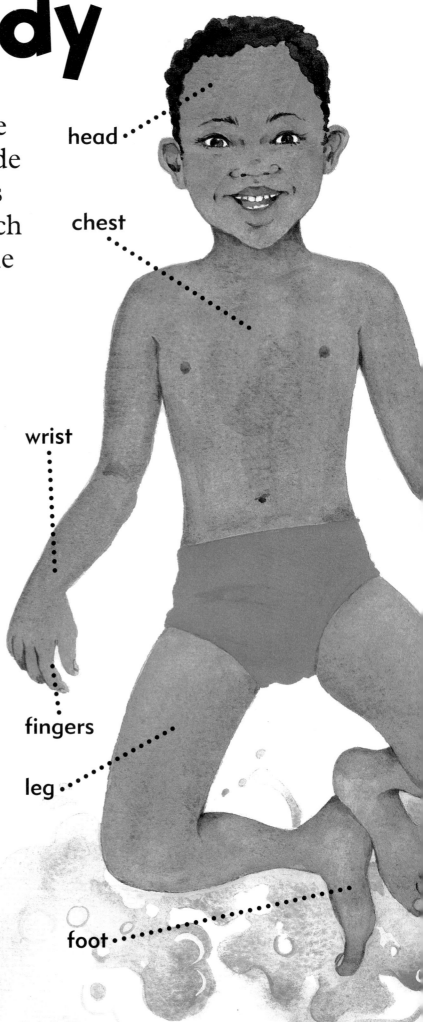

head

chest

wrist

fingers

leg

foot

A baby holds his mother's hands and learns to walk for the first time. Soon, he will be able to walk all on his own.

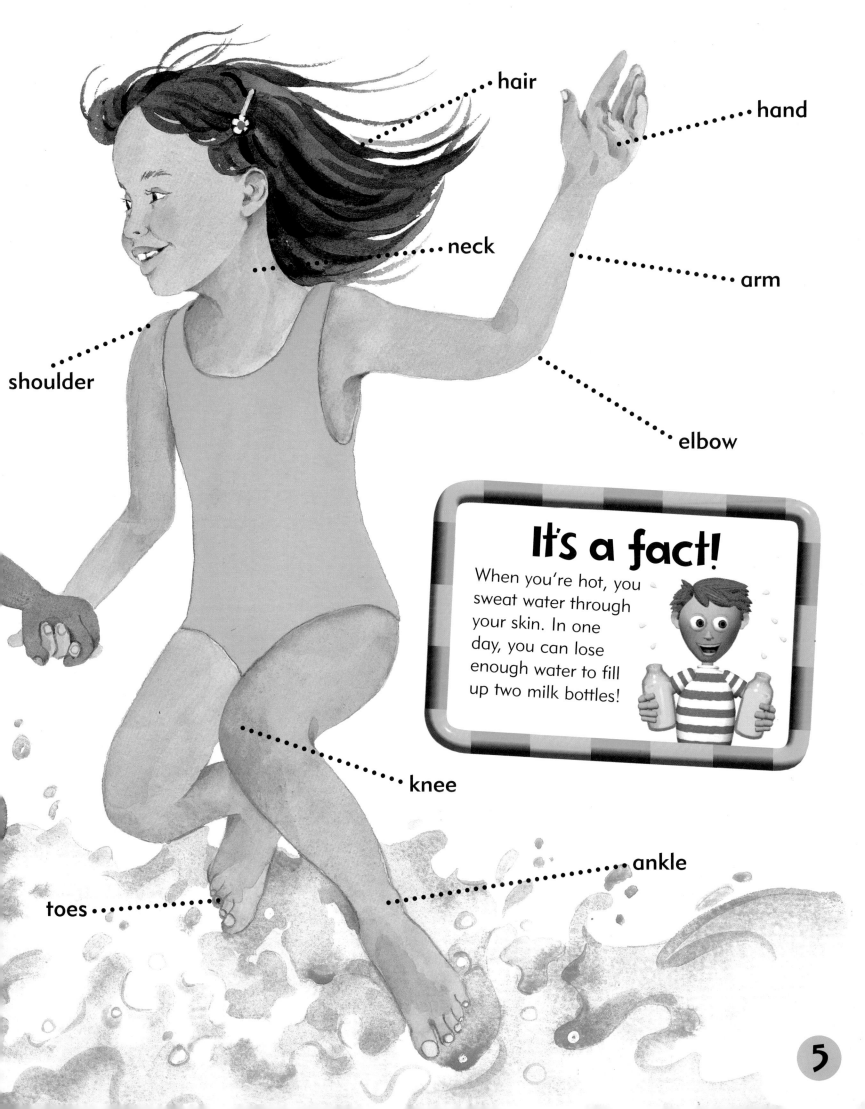

hair

hand

neck

arm

shoulder

elbow

It's a fact!

When you're hot, you sweat water through your skin. In one day, you can lose enough water to fill up two milk bottles!

knee

ankle

toes

5

Bones

Inside your body, you have hundreds of hard bones that are different shapes and sizes. They all join up to make a big, strong frame, called a skeleton. Try tapping your knee. Can you feel the bones underneath your skin?

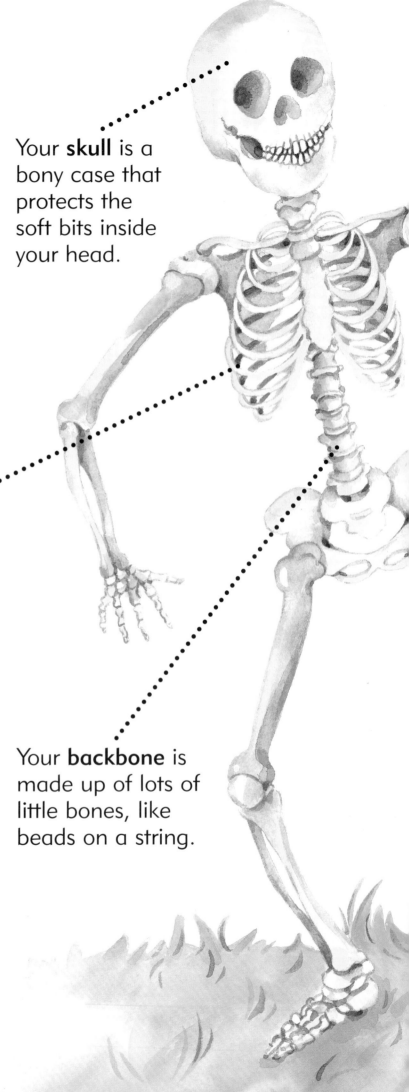

Your **skull** is a bony case that protects the soft bits inside your head.

Two rows of curvy **ribs** make a large cage around your chest.

Your **backbone** is made up of lots of little bones, like beads on a string.

These skaters are whizzing quickly along a path. They wear helmets and pads to protect their bones if they fall.

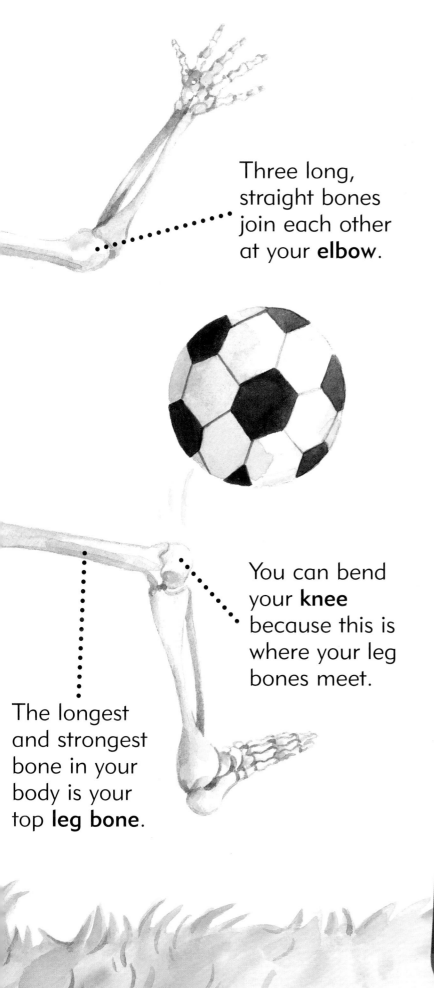

Three long, straight bones join each other at your **elbow**.

You can bend your **knee** because this is where your leg bones meet.

The longest and strongest bone in your body is your top **leg bone**.

Luckily, broken bones are easy to mend. A doctor wraps them in a stiff plaster cast, then they grow together again.

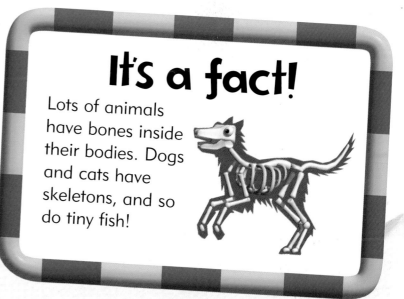

It's a fact!

Lots of animals have bones inside their bodies. Dogs and cats have skeletons, and so do tiny fish!

Run and jump

Strong muscles under your skin help you to bend and stretch your body. You use muscles every time you shake your head, wiggle a toe or jump up and down. The big picture shows children playing leapfrog. This game uses lots of muscles!

It's a fact!

Exercise makes your muscles stronger. Some men make their muscles so strong, they can lift up a car.

Bend your back and try to curl up into a round ball.

Pull your knees up towards your head as far as they will go.

Dancing is a really fun way to exercise your body. Everybody tries to move their arms and legs in the same way!

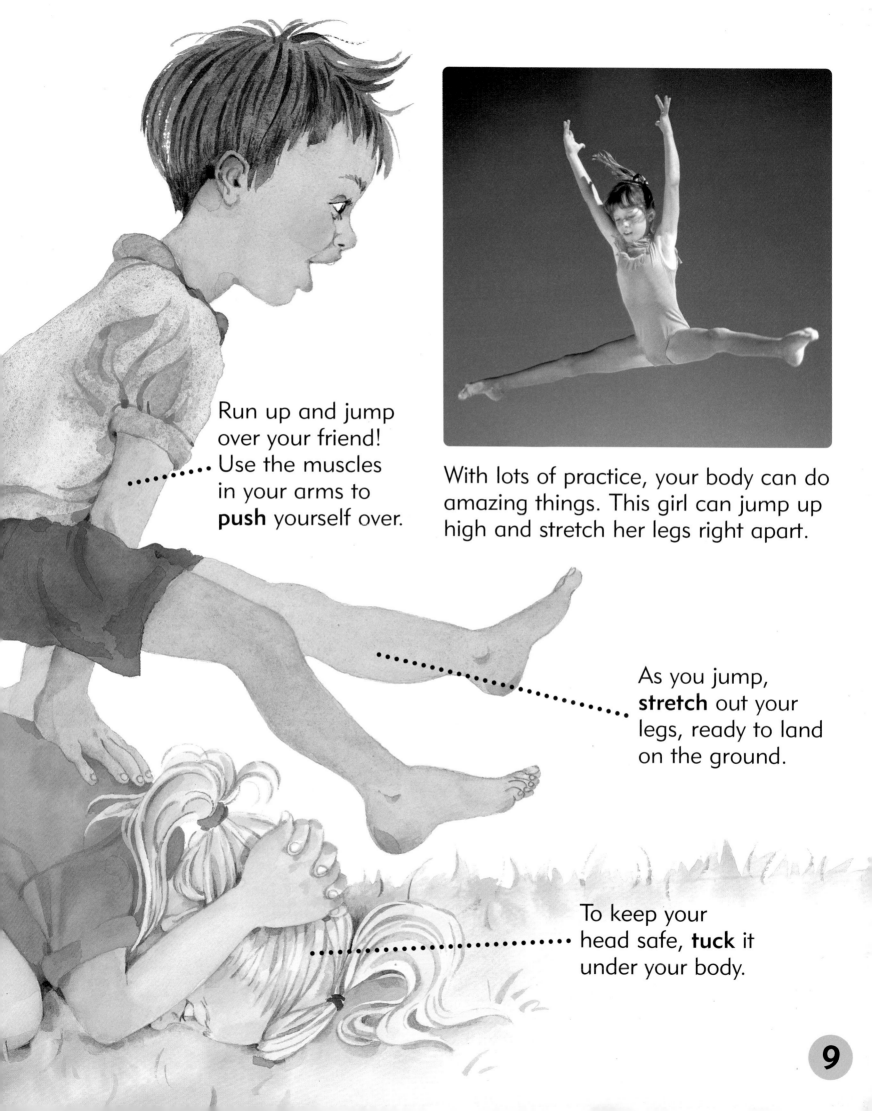

Run up and jump over your friend! Use the muscles in your arms to **push** yourself over.

With lots of practice, your body can do amazing things. This girl can jump up high and stretch her legs right apart.

As you jump, **stretch** out your legs, ready to land on the ground.

To keep your head safe, **tuck** it under your body.

9

 Inside my body

Your body is packed full of soft parts, called organs, that do extremely important jobs. They help you to breathe, to eat, and even to think. There's also a lot of thick blood inside your body. It carries food around, from your head to your toes.

Your **brain** is inside your head. It helps you to think and learn.

When you breathe out underwater, you can see air come out of your mouth and nose in huge, shiny bubbles!

10

Every time you breathe in, two spongy bags, called **lungs**, fill up with air.

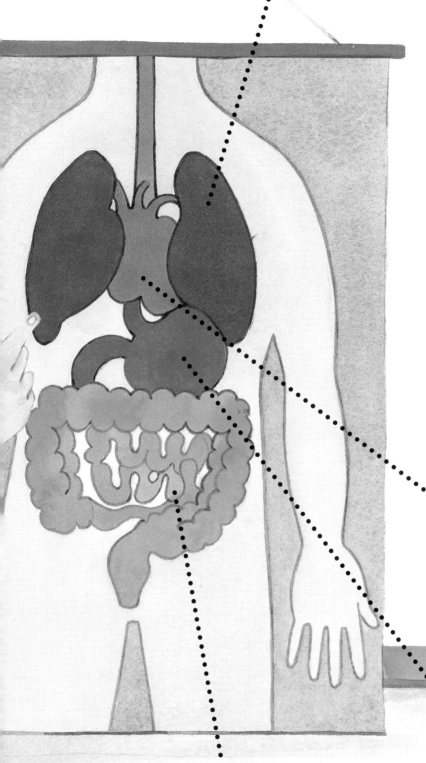

Doctors use this instrument to listen to your heart beating inside your chest. It sounds like a drum. Thump! Thump!

Your **heart** pumps blood around your body all day and all night.

Your wiggly **gut** soaks up the best bits of food. The rest of it slides to the end and you go to the toilet!

Your **stomach** churns up all the food you eat into a mushy soup.

Playing in the park

The park is full of children playing different games. They bend and stretch their bodies in all sorts of ways!

12

How is the girl making her friend swing high up in the sky?

Which parts of her body does the girl bend to pick up the stick?

Words you know

Here are some words that you learned earlier. Say them out loud, then try finding the things in the picture.

knee   elbow   leg

shoulder   chest   arm

13

What are the two boys throwing and catching?

My face

Everyone's face is different! Your face is the part of your body that shows people how you feel inside. Crying can mean that you are feeling sad, smiling shows everyone that you are happy.

You use your **eyes** to look at the world around you.

Thick, curly **eyelashes** stop specks of dirt from getting into your eyes.

When you are happy, your **mouth** curls up into a big smile!

These brothers are identical twins. They were born on the same day and look almost exactly the same as each other.

Hair grows curly or straight. It might be red, brown, yellow or black.

You can hear soft sounds and loud sounds with your **ears**.

Your **nose** tells you if a smell is nice or nasty.

Strong, rock-hard **teeth** are for biting and chewing food.

It's a fact!

If you do not cut your hair, it may keep growing until it trails behind you on the ground!

 # See and hear

All day long, you look at things around you and hear all sorts of sounds. You do it without even trying! The three children in the big picture are playing music and singing at the tops of their voices. Do you like listening to music?

This girl is wearing **glasses** to help her to see more clearly.

These children can talk with their hands. They can't hear words so they make special signs to each other.

If you practise hard, you can learn to play a tune on a **recorder**.

When you look through a magnifying glass, everything seems really big – even the patterns on a little butterfly's wings.

It's easy to **sing** along to the music when you know the words.

As you sing, try to **clap** your hands in time with the music.

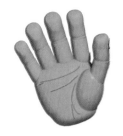

Touch and feel

Does a feather feel soft or hard, smooth or rough? You find out how things feel by touching them. Your fingertips are best for touching but toes are good, too. The big picture shows lots of things you can find on a beach. Can you imagine how they feel?

When you dig your feet into sand, the tiny grains **tickle** between your toes.

Rock is hard and jagged. It feels **rough** against your bare skin.

It's a fact!

Your body hates to be cold. You shiver and shake until your teeth rattle and your nose turns blue!

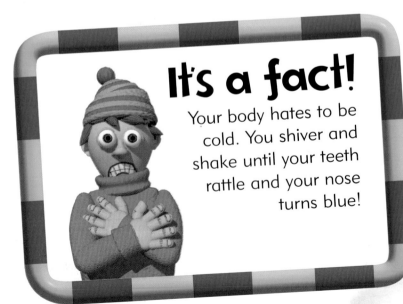

Seaweed feels **slimy** when it's wet. It slips through your fingers.

This boy loves his pet dog. He presses his face against the dog's soft, furry coat to give him a big hug.

On a hot day, it feels good to dip your hand in the **cool** sea water.

Keep away from a sea urchin or it will sting you with its **prickly** spines!

 # Taste and smell

Your tongue does a special job. When you eat, it tells you if your food tastes nice or horrid. Your nose helps, too, by catching smells that float up into the air. The smell of fresh popcorn or hot pizza can make you feel really hungry.

Licking an ice-cream makes your tongue tingle. It feels really cold in your mouth but tastes yummy!

Biscuits and cakes are made with lots of sugar to make them taste **sweet**.

Lemons taste so **sour** that eating them makes you screw up your face!

20

Crisps and peanuts are **salty**. You want a drink after eating them.

Steaming, hot pizza **smells** so good that you can't wait to eat it.

A fresh flower smells lovely. Holding it close to your nose is the best way to sniff its special scent.

21

 Keeping well

Your body is a wonderful machine – just think of all the things it can do. But you must look after it to stay healthy. You need plenty of exercise, water, fresh food and sleep. Don't forget to wash each day to keep yourself clean!

Fresh fruit is really good for you. It tastes delicious and even helps your body to grow.

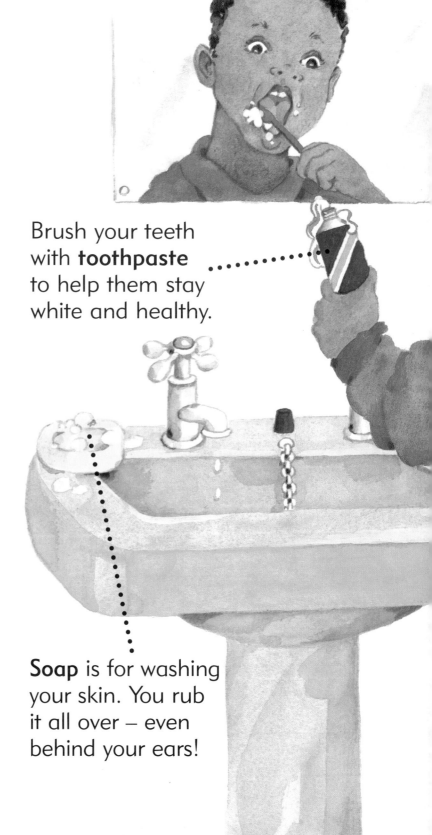

Brush your teeth with **toothpaste** to help them stay white and healthy.

Soap is for washing your skin. You rub it all over – even behind your ears!

22

If you cut your skin, wear a **plaster** to keep it clean while it mends.

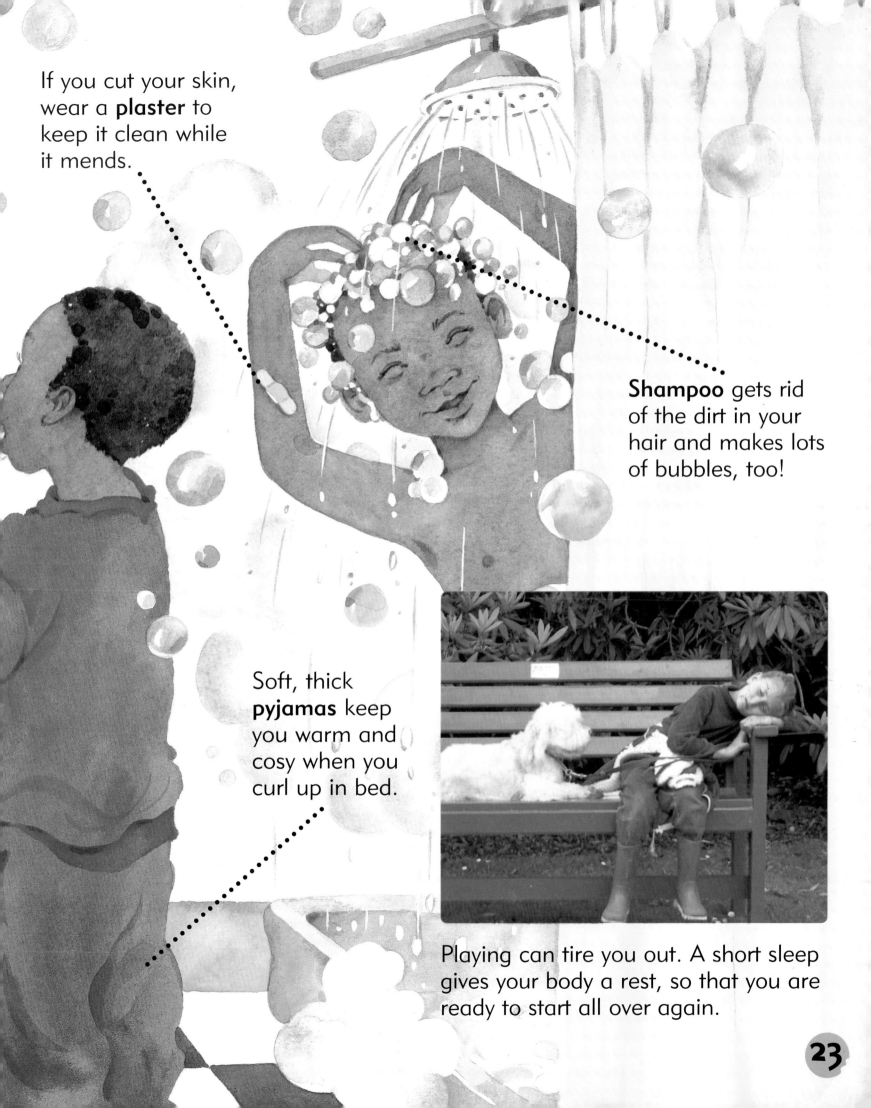

Shampoo gets rid of the dirt in your hair and makes lots of bubbles, too!

Soft, thick **pyjamas** keep you warm and cosy when you curl up in bed.

Playing can tire you out. A short sleep gives your body a rest, so that you are ready to start all over again.

Fun at the beach

On a hot day, lots of people go to the beach. It's fun to sit on the warm sand or to splash about in the sea.

24

Words you know

Here are some words that you learned earlier. Say them out loud, then try finding the things in the picture.

mouth	eyes	nose
teeth	hair	ears

Life Guard

Which boy is listening to music from a radio?

Sam's big surprise

One day, Sam's mum said that she was going to have a baby. Sam was very excited but he had one pet hate, and that was...waiting!

When Sam's dad baked a cake, as soon as he took the mixing bowl out, Sam said, "Is it nearly ready?"

And when Sam found out that he had to wait, his face went bright red and he shouted, "I *can't* wait!"

When Sam's grandma took Sam on an outing, as soon as they set off, Sam said, "Are we nearly there?"

And when Sam found out that he had to wait, his face went bright red and he shouted, "I *can't* wait!"

Everyone just smiled at Sam as they watched his face turn redder and redder and said, "Sam Tate, you have to wait. There are some things you just can't hurry!"

Sam hated waiting for the new baby. When he gently touched his mum's tummy, he felt the baby kicking inside!

Every day he said, "Will the baby be born today?" but his mum just smiled at him and said, "Remember Sam Tate, sometimes you have to wait."

One morning, Sam found his dad packing a bag while his mum was sitting by the front door.

"We have to go to the hospital," said Dad, "the baby will be born today."

The second Sam heard this, he raced down the stairs and jumped up and down in front of his mum. "When will you be home?" asked Sam.

Then, he found out that he had to wait. His face went bright red, and he shouted, "I *can't* wait!"

"This is worth waiting for," said Mum, and gave him a big hug.

"Be good," called Dad, as they hurried outside to the car.

Sam stood at the window and watched his mum and dad drive away. "I *can't* wait," he mumbled to himself and his face turned redder and redder.

Sam soon felt bored standing by the window so he went to look for Grandma and Grandpa. He found them in the baby's nursery.

"While we wait," said Grandma, "we'll get the baby's room ready. When babies are small, they can only lie in their cots, so they need things to look at."

Sam sat down and opened up a magazine that lay on the floor. It was full of pictures of things for babies.

"Wow!" shouted Sam, pointing at a picture of a huge mobile. There were lots of paper aeroplanes dangling from strings. "Can we get one of these?" he asked.

"Oh dear, it's a bit late. The baby will be here tomorrow," said Grandma. "Never mind, we have lots of other things," and she pulled a baby's rattle out of a box.

"Can I have the box?" asked Sam.

"What for?" said Grandma.

"Just to play with," said Sam.

27

"It's a surprise," said Sam.

And with that, he picked up the magazine, the box, the tape and the cotton, and hurried out of the nursery.

"What is he up to?" said Grandpa, watching him go into his bedroom and shut the door.

"Search me!" said Grandma.

A little while later, Sam's grandpa was painting animal shapes on the nursery door. He wondered what Sam was doing, so he tiptoed across the landing and pressed his ear against Sam's bedroom door. He nearly jumped out of his skin when Sam suddenly opened it.

"I was just wondering if your door needed painting, too," muttered Grandpa.

"Can I have some paint?" asked Sam.

Grandpa gave Sam the tin of paint and Sam said thank you. Then he went back into his bedroom and closed the door.

Sam stayed in his room all afternoon. He only came out when it was time for tea. He had sticky tape in his hair, paint on his face and pieces of cotton hanging off his T-shirt.

"Look at the mess you're in!" said Sam's grandma. "What have you been doing?"

Sam just grinned and said, "It's a big surprise."

Later on, Sam watched his grandpa stick two long, brightly coloured friezes all round the wall.

"Can I have some tape?" asked Sam.

"What for?" asked Grandpa.

"Oh, it's just for a game," said Sam.

Then, Sam helped his grandma to unpack a large bag full of baby toys. He pulled out a soft, stripy tiger.

"That was your favourite toy when you were a baby, but it's falling apart," said Grandma. "Let's see if I can sew it back together again."

She asked Sam to fetch her sewing basket and her glasses. When Sam came back, he asked if he could have some cotton.

"What for?" asked Grandma.

Not long after it got dark, the telephone rang – Sam's grandma and grandpa fell over each other trying to answer it. It was Sam's dad calling to say that Sam had a little baby sister, and that they were coming home in the morning.

As soon as Sam heard that he had a sister, his face went red, he jumped up and down and he shouted, "I can't wait!"

"It won't be for long," said Grandma, "but now it's time for bed. You must be tired out!"

Sam put on his pyjamas, then he brushed his teeth and washed his grubby face. He climbed into bed and Grandpa and Grandma gave him a hug, then they turned out the light. A minute later, Sam tiptoed out of his room, holding something in his hands. He disappeared into the nursery for a moment, then crept back into his bedroom.

The next morning, Sam was standing at the window, waiting for his mum and dad to arrive with his new sister.

"They're here, they're here!" shouted Sam when he spotted the car.

Sam flung open the door and his dad came in first, holding a tiny bundle in his arms. He bent down to show Sam. And Sam saw a little red face, with tightly closed eyes. And two little pink, wrinkled hands which were opening and closing.

Sam couldn't believe how tiny the baby's hands were. She had tiny, pink fingernails too. Her skin was the softest thing that Sam had ever felt.

"She looks angry," said Sam, peering at his sister's crumpled face.

"She looks just like you do when you say you can't wait," laughed Dad.

"Will you bring her upstairs?" said Sam. "We've got a surprise for her."

Everyone went upstairs and Sam opened the nursery door.

Sam's mum and dad were amazed to see the colourful friezes all round the wall, the animal paintings on the door and all the baby toys. But most of all, they admired a large mobile that was hanging next to the cot.

"So that's what you were doing all day," said Grandpa. "You were making a surprise present for your new sister!"

"Oh," said Mum, "it looks beautiful, Sam. Thank you very much."

"It must have taken you ages to make!" said Dad.

By now, the baby was fast asleep so Sam's mum put her in the cot.

"Well, was she worth waiting for?" asked Sam's dad.

"Oh yes," said Sam. "Can I hold her?"

"Wait till she wakes up," said Mum.

When she said that, Sam's face started to go red.

"Are you going to shout..." said Dad, "...or are you going to come downstairs to see our surprise for you?"

Sam quickly closed his mouth and followed his mum and dad downstairs. There, on the kitchen table, was a big box of paints.

"Wow!" shouted Sam, jumping up and down. "Now I can paint lots of pictures for my sister's room. I can't wait!"

30

Puzzles

Double trouble!

These two pictures show a boy kicking a football. Can you spot four differences between the pictures?

a

b

Close up!

Here are some children you have seen in this book but they are in close up. Can you tell what they're doing?

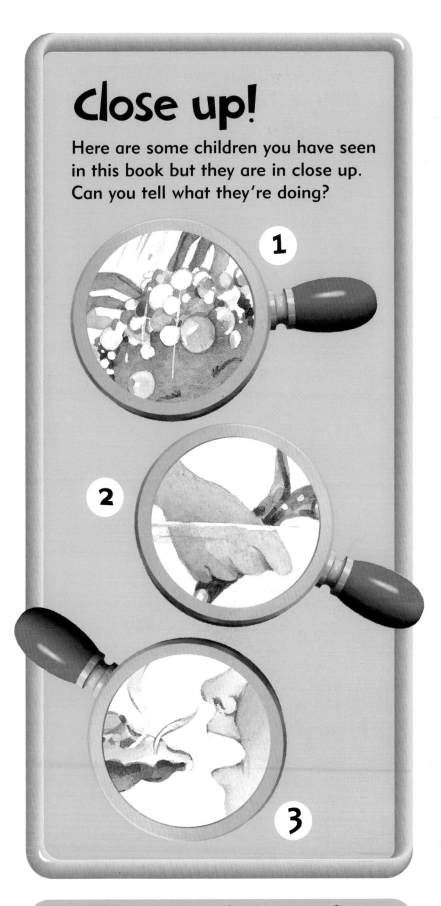

1

2

3

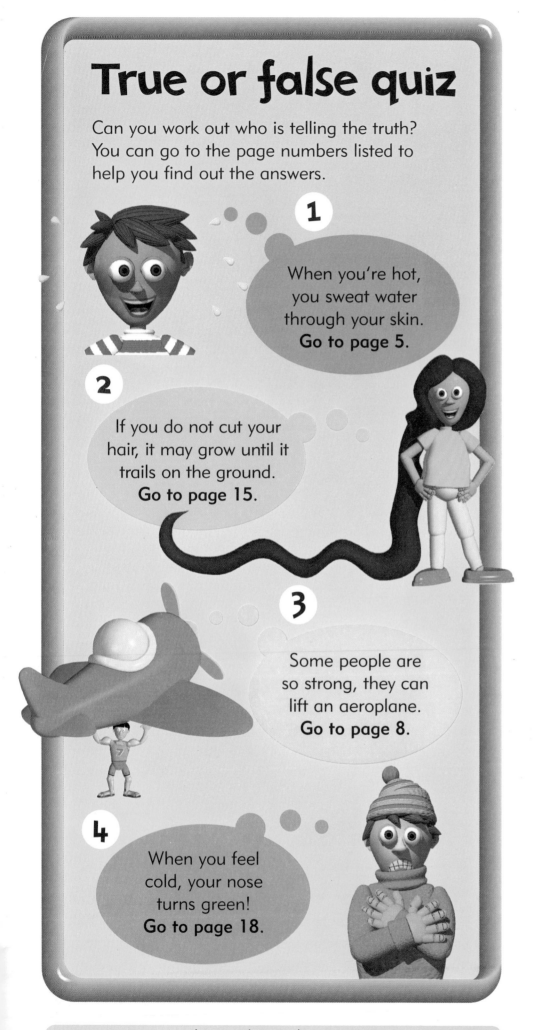

True or false quiz

Can you work out who is telling the truth? You can go to the page numbers listed to help you find out the answers.

1 When you're hot, you sweat water through your skin. **Go to page 5.**

2 If you do not cut your hair, it may grow until it trails on the ground. **Go to page 15.**

3 Some people are so strong, they can lift an aeroplane. **Go to page 8.**

4 When you feel cold, your nose turns green! **Go to page 18.**

Answers: 1 true, 2 true, 3 false, 4 false.

Index

arm 5, 8, 9, 13

bones 6, 7

breathing 10, 11

ears 15, 25

eating 10, 11, 20, 21

elbow 5, 7, 13

eyes 14, 25

fingers 4, 18, 19

foot 4, 18

hair 5, 15, 23, 25

hand 4, 5, 16, 17, 19

knee 5, 6, 7, 8, 13

leg 4, 7, 8, 9, 13

mouth 10, 14, 20, 25

muscles 8, 9

nose 10, 15, 18, 20, 21, 25

skin 4, 5, 6, 8, 18, 22

sleeping 22, 23, 24

teeth 15, 18, 22, 25

toes 5, 8, 10, 18

tongue 20, 25

washing 22, 23